T0034729

Reaching for Starlight

Also by Donna-Michelle St. Bernard

Cake

Gas Girls

Indian Act: Residential School Plays (editor)

A Man A Fish

Refractions: Scenes (edited with Yvette Nolan)

Refractions: Solo (edited with Yvette Nolan)

Sound of the Beast

Reaching for Starlight

by Donna-Michelle St. Bernard

Playwrights Canada Press
Toronto

Reaching for Starlight © Copyright 2023 by Donna-Michelle St. Bernard
First edition: January 2023
Printed and bound in Canada by Rapido Books, Montreal

Jacket art, *Mint Green Bantu Knots*, by Shellicka Anglin
Author photo © Denise Grant

Playwrights Canada Press
202-269 Richmond St. W., Toronto, ON M5V 1X1
416.703.0013 | info@playwrightscanada.com | www.playwrightscanada.com

No part of this book may be reproduced, downloaded, or used in any form or by any means without the prior written permission of the publisher, except for excerpts in a review or by a licence from Access Copyright, www.accesscopyright.ca.

For professional or amateur production rights, please contact:
Michael Petrasek, Kensington Literary Representation
34 St. Andrew Street, Toronto, ON M5T 1K6
416.848.9648 | kensingtonlit@rogers.com

LIBRARY AND ARCHIVES CANADA CATALOGUING IN PUBLICATION
Title: Reaching for starlight / Donna-Michelle St. Bernard.
Names: St. Bernard, Donna-Michelle, author.
Description: A play.
Identifiers: Canadiana (print) 20220430705 | Canadiana (ebook) 20220430721
  | ISBN 9780369103888 (softcover) | ISBN 9780369103901 (PDF)
  | ISBN 9780369103895 (EPUB)
Classification: LCC PS8637.A4525 R43 2022 | DDC C812/.6—dc23

Playwrights Canada Press operates on land which is the ancestral home of the Anishinaabe Nations (Ojibwe / Chippewa, Odawa, Potawatomi, Algonquin, Saulteaux, Nipissing, and Mississauga), the Wendat, and the members of the Haudenosaunee Confederacy (Mohawk, Oneida, Onondaga, Cayuga, Seneca, and Tuscarora), as well as Metis and Inuit peoples. It always was and always will be Indigenous land.

We acknowledge the support of the Canada Council for the Arts, the Ontario Arts Council (OAC), Ontario Creates, and the Government of Canada for our publishing activities.

For Black girls with aspirations and those who challenge, encourage, teach, and learn from them.

Inspired by loving lineages:
Brenda, Andi, Savi.
Ntombi, Warona, Khaya.
Claudette, Jan, Hannah.

So, it goes . . .

Foreword

by Mike Payette

Our encounters in creating and sharing our stories within a mainstream / mainstage (i.e., institutional) theatre platform have historically been complicated and layered with the internal struggle of accommodating a "universal" audience. At the time of my first conversation with Donna-Michelle about what would become *Reaching for Starlight*, I was early in my transition as Artistic and Executive Director of Geordie Productions, a true leader in Theatre for Young Audiences (TYA) within English-language Quebec. I was excited to have a space to explore what it meant for a lauded company to deepen its work emboldening stories by voices that were not as represented and to foster an environment of access to *all* young people and their families. The "how" was a continuous investigation and required deep internal and organizational reflection and action—yet, in truth, empowering the storytellers who shape the stories we seek was an easy start.

There is no default in universality and that is what makes theatre so engaging because it is, in fact, a mirror to all the complexities within the scope of humanity's intersectionality, difference, and beauty. The importance of paving a path for *all* young people to envision themselves as unique and powerful in a world that they are just starting to grapple with is a huge driving force of so many TYA practitioners. It is one of the most rewarding aspects of TYA creation, and the audience—some of the wisest and honest folx—remain the focus of inspiration. In the end, we are guiding and uplifting through the art of storytelling—a tremendous responsibility.

For nearly three years, Donna-Michelle and I embarked on a creative process that actively encouraged Black kids to experience a highly artistic exchange between theatre and the physical world, and to raise an investigation of what it means to find agency within a system that often discourages them from embracing—in the case of Reenie and Maya—their Black girl magic.

That's a lot to drop in at a young age. My stepdaughter, Khaya, is now the age of Reenie and Maya within the play, and I am amazed, yet unsurprised, by the scope of her questioning years before that. Seriously, I would just be moved by how she would listen to conversations, how she would filter and decipher in a way that she could hold onto. At five to six years old, Khaya was already in the midst of processing the world around her and her place within it. And let's be real, as we adults try to make up for the world's calamities and injustices, our kids are the ones looking up and looking for supportive anchors on top of the noise.

As many great convos and moments happen, the seed of this piece began during storytime with Khaya and her mama, Warona, reading Kristy Dempsey and Floyd Cooper's *A Dance Like Starlight*, which told the story of a young Black girl and her seamstress mom who saw Janet Collins perform in the thick of 1950s America. The message was simple— dreams can be realized.

Coincidentally, at the time of its development, *Reaching for Starlight* was given the backdrop of so many stories within the ballet world—a world that has often been regarded as protectionist regarding how and which bodies were allowed to partake—that were showing signs of some progress. The introduction of brown ballet shoes, the breakout of Misty Copeland, the introduction of ballet/hip hop fusion, and more culturally diverse dancers within our largest classical institutions in North America . . . evolution continues to happen.

The prize of this creation journey, however, was honouring Reenie's journey as a strong, funny, and inquisitive young person. She is uncomfortable with accepting anything just for the sake of it, and that comes with its own challenges, but her spirit and search for justice is what makes her a steward for change within a system she has grown accustomed to but is now learning where the gaps are that ensure access to everyone. She is a part of the legacy of so many heroic young pioneers.

I think back to the many voices and bodies who contributed to the artistic discourse of this piece and for the care Donna-Michelle placed in holding the young voice to the pinnacle of respect and awe. Works like these inspire us adults to remember the wisdom of young people, and how we are all universally affected by the uniqueness of one's own journey. It reminds the younger versions of artists like myself, Donna-Michelle, and all those involved to be re-ignited by our awesomeness and to lift the voice of our younger selves to a higher esteem. This is where we collectively grow while celebrating the breadth of *all* the voices that make our world vibrant, complicated, and beautiful.

Mike Payette is an award-winning director, educator, and actor who has appeared with some of Canada's finest theatres, including the Citadel, Vertigo, Banff Centre, Segal Centre, Centaur, the Grand, Factory, Neptune, and the National Arts Centre. A frequent guest artist at the National Theatre School of Canada, some of his memorable works as a director include Harlem Duet *(Black Theatre Workshop),* Hosanna *(Tableau D'Hôte Theatre / Centaur),* Around the World in 80 Days *and* Reaching for Starlight *(Geordie Theatre), the Canadian premiere of Tarell Alvin McCraney's* Choir Boy *(Centaur, later with Canadian Stage / Arts Club),* Cockroach *(Tarragon),* Sensitivity *(Obsidian Theatre / CBC Gem, as part of 21* Black Futures*), the Quebec premiere of* Héritage (A Raisin in the Sun) *(Théâtre Duceppe), along with national tours of* The Tashme Project *(Tashme Prod / Centaur / Factory / Firehall) and Lorena Gale's* Angélique *(Black Theatre Workshop / Tableau D'Hôte / National Arts Centre / Factory / Obsidian). He was the co-founding artistic director of Tableau D'Hôte Theatre, past assistant artistic director for Black Theatre Workshop, and was the artistic and executive director of Geordie Theatre before becoming artistic director of Tarragon Theatre in Toronto, where he now resides.*

Reaching for Starlight was written in response to *A Dance Like Starlight* by Kristy Dempsey and Floyd Cooper, and was commissioned by Geordie Productions and developed with support from Geordie Theatre and Playwrights' Workshop Montréal. The play was nominated for Outstanding New Text at the 2018/2019 Montreal English Theatre Awards in its first production by Geordie Productions at Geordie Theatre, Montreal, from April 26 to May 5, 2019, with the following cast and creative team:

Cast: Samantha Bitonti, Shawn Campbell, Curtis Legault, Bria McLaughlin, Keren Roberts, Anana Rydvald, Sarah Segal-Lazar, Warona Setshwaelo, Geneviève Smith-Courtois, Dakota Jamal Wellman, Jane Wheeler, and Jenna Wheeler-Hughes.

Directed by Mike Payette
Choreographed by Véronique Gaudreau
Dramaturgy by Mike Payette and Emma Tibaldo
Set and Costumes Design by Cathia Pagotto
Lighting Design by Tim Rodrigues
Sound Design by Rob Denton

Production Team: Amy-Susie Bradford, Danielle Skene, Holly Hilts, Shanti Gonzales, Katey Wattam, Marianne Lavoie, Nalo Soyini Bruce, Sarah Mauracher, Þórhildur Sunna Jóhannsdóttir, Dil Hildebrand, Acosta, Audrey Lee, Nikita Bala, and Geri Weir.

Characters

Reenie: Athletic. Imaginative. Afr.
Lil: Mother of Reenie. Afr.
Maia: Junior Ensemble member. Afr.
Jo: Junior Ensemble member.
Pops: Father of Jo.
Maestra: Ballet instructor.
Dawn: Junior Ensemble member.
Karyn: Junior Ensemble member.
Dafonte: Brother of Maia. Afr.

Settings

Studio: ballet studio / classroom / Maestra's domain.
Waiting Area: outside studio / parents' and guardians' domain.
City: commute route between studio and home.
Home: Reenie and Lil's apartment.

Style Notes

Maestra uses a trick of the mirror to visually implicate herself among the ensemble during sequences.

Good Hair: There is a discernible difference between Maia's hair and Reenie's, whether it is style or texture. Maia has braids. Reenie's hair can be straightened or natural, but should be combable (should be determined in discussion with the actor, with consideration for their comfort).

Clapping Code: One clap = starting positions / barre. Two claps = begin choreographed sequence. Three claps = dance freely. Snap = you know what you did, go impose the appropriate punishment on yourself. Gesture = dismissal.

Commute Transition: These movement sequences involve the entire cast as members of the general public, except where specific roles are indicated.

Fire Escape: Reenie's fortress of solitude, which allows her imagination to transform into a superhero looking over the city. Also referred to by Reenie as "lurking."

Sequence: A choreo routine that the class is learning.

Prelude

Movement: community. Flash mob street scene. Traffic, com-muters, taxis hailed, bus riders, space being shared, negotiated.

Pitted

Ballet studio.
Ensemble enters.
Occasional voice: "Excuse me. / Hi. / Two, three, four . . . "
They stretch at the barre,
performing intense internal focus,
but each is acutely aware of each other's aptitude/shortcomings.
Someone casually pops up en pointe,
someone else casually pops up tighter, taller.
They run through warm-ups.
DAWN gets a cheese string from her bag.

DAWN: Well, I'm finished.

MAIA: You're gonna be finished if Maestra catches you eating in here.

DAWN: Want some?

KARYN: No way!

JO: You've got twenty seconds.

DAWN hides the wrapper. REENIE mimics MAESTRA, claps.

REENIE: "Children! I expect precision, perfection, poise . . . and punctuality!"

MAESTRA enters right on time.
There is an intake of breath, a straightening of posture, silence.
MAESTRA goes down the line inspecting and correcting postures.

MAESTRA: Maia, is that a hole in your leotard? Unacceptable. Get it fixed by next week or buy a new one downstairs. And . . .

MAESTRA claps once. Ensemble takes up starting positions.

Silence, now. Hear each other. Breathe as one. Move as one. Listen.

MAESTRA claps twice. Ensemble dances "Sequence." MAESTRA singles out KARYN for praise.

Brava, ma petite. Brava. Together, children. Together. I need to see those lines. Give me clean, orderly, intentional lines. Yes! Yes! Allons y, mes chères.

As the class sweeps arms upwards, REENIE throws a dab. The ensemble giggles. MAESTRA frowns. LIL watches through the window in the parents' waiting area. POPS arrives. "Sequence" comes to its conclusion. MAESTRA claps twice.

POPS: They still going?

LIL: There's five minutes left in the class.

POPS: Aw, c'mon. Dance faster.

LIL: Watch this. Jo's got a sweet moment in this section.

POPS: Real sweet, way in the back there.

LIL checks her phone, sees a text.

LIL: Excuse me. I have to make a call.

LIL steps out. MAESTRA claps once. Ensemble returns to starting positions. MAESTRA reveals The Firebird *concept image.*

MAESTRA: Well done, children. Now, before you go, I have selected the piece for the year-end recital. You will dance . . . *The Firebird.*

Suppressed gasps from the ensemble.

It's not an easy one, but it is a classic. It will be gruelling. You will work, you will sweat, you will undoubtedly cry, but then you will suck it up and achieve. By all rights you should train at least another ten years before you dare attempt Stravinsky, but I can get you there. I'm that good.

DAWN: That all sounds hard.

MAESTRA: Is someone speaking in my studio? You're on notice, Dawn. Children. Do you want to live a life of no chances taken? No glory pursued? Do you want to do *The Nutcracker* every year for the rest of your life, or will you endeavour, now, to pull off a miracle?

JO: Yes! A miracle!

MAESTRA: No, I'm not looking for your thoughts, thank you. Mine are excellent. What I need is for you to do exactly as you are told. Do you understand? . . . Respond!

ALL: Yes, ma'am!

MAESTRA: Well done, all of you.

> *MAESTRA claps thrice. Ensemble breaks into a freestyle dance break—this is a treat, and where we can see the ensemble's styles individuate. MAESTRA snaps and points to REENIE. REENIE reacts.*

Reenie, you know what you did.

> *Resigned, REENIE performs a routine drill as punishment for her disruption—sauté/relevé/répète, interminably.*

Remember, children: inhabit the impossible.

> *MAESTRA claps once.*

Your free hour begins now. You may use this time in the studio as you please. You are not required to stay . . . Unless you are truly dedicated to excellence.

> *MAIA, REENIE, and KARYN stay. DAWN leaves. LIL enters and hands an envelope to MAESTRA.*

LIL: Here you go, Maestra. Registration forms and fees. Now if only I could get the rest of my life in order.

MAESTRA: Yes. Well. Discipline is a gift we give ourselves, isn't it?

LIL: Yes.

MAESTRA: You know, Reenie really is quite gifted. She just needs to work on her behaviour.

LIL: Tell me about it.

LIL helps REENIE get her things together to leave. POPS goes in and has a word with MAESTRA. JO waits beside them.

POPS: So, is Jo gonna dance the solo this year like we talked about?

MAESTRA: You talked about. I have not yet decided.

POPS: What's to decide, Catherine?

JO: It's okay. I don't mind, either way.

POPS: It's not about whether you mind, Jo—

JO: I like being Ensemble.

POPS: Listen, if you wanna keep doing this, you have to distinguish yourself. That's the deal.

LIL returns. POPS turns to MAESTRA, raising his voice.

Let me ask you something: Are any of these other kids legacy?

POPS lowers his voice.

Excuse me. Are they? Are they legacy? Are any of them third generation? Did their grandmothers dance for the governor general at the Chatham County Bicentennial? Because that used to mean something.

MAESTRA: I have not yet decided.

MAESTRA exits. POPS turns to JO.

POPS: And you. You wanna get pushed around your whole life? Learn to stand up for yourself.

Outside, LIL adjusts REENIE's scarf for better coverage.
REENIE tries to shrug off LIL's hands.

LIL: So . . .

REENIE: So?

LIL: Any news?

REENIE: Um, I think there's still a refugee crisis. Probably some weather somewhere.

LIL: Mm. Okay. How was class?

REENIE: Same.

LIL: Exactly the same? What a waste. And to think I spend my hard-earned / money [on that class].

REENIE: Okay! Not the same. The worst, actually. Totally unfair.

LIL: "Um," how about you tell me.

REENIE: "Um," how about Reenie does repetitive nonsense while everyone else does free dance? "Sauté, relevé. Sauté, relevé." How about that?

LIL pretends to commiserate.

LIL: And all just because . . .

REENIE: Yeah, all just because of one little mischief in the overture.

LIL: That's wild. It's almost as if you knew the rules, you chose to break them, and now you have to live with the completely predictable consequences. What a world.

REENIE: You're literally the worst.

LIL: I know, right? Despite your refusal to take this seriously, I noticed your extension is stronger than ever. Now, if I was casting the year-end recital, that's the kind of power I'd want to see in a solo.

REENIE: I guess. Who knows.

LIL: Well, with an extension like that, I might make you the whole show. Am I right?

REENIE: Mom. What's a legacy?

LIL: It's what you leave behind. What you stood for, how you'll be remembered. Like if you were the first to do something, or the best.

REENIE: Then how does Jo already have it? He's eleven.

LIL: Well, for some it's what you leave behind, and for some it's what gets handed to you. Some folks get to pick up where their parents left off.

REENIE: So, a head start?

LIL: I guess it looks that way.

REENIE: Do I have a legacy?

LIL: Sure. Your ever see your granny squint and tilt her head kinda sideways?

REENIE imitates Granny. LIL does too.

Right. That's your legacy.

REENIE: Oh, great.

LIL: You should be proud of your granny's little squint. Cuz when we go see the ballet, see all the princesses and soldiers and swans and rats on the stage, we know that way down in the basement there's a dark little room they hardly use anymore. And down in that room your grandma used to make all those pretty costumes. Sequin after sequin. By hand. Part of her was there, in every single piece she created. She was really good.

REENIE: So if that's our legacy, how come you don't sew costumes?

LIL: Cuz legacy is just a place to start. You still have to do something with it.

REENIE: Like?

LIL: Like, your granny got us into the building.

REENIE: Into the basement.

LIL: Right. And your good-looking mom took it further, got herself up those stairs, into the rehearsal studio. And my amazing kid is gonna be up there, centre stage, picking up where I left off, and taking it all the way.

REENIE: Yeah, okay. Sounds like a long way to go, though. Mom, can I put in my earphones, please?

LIL: Okay, sure.

> *LIL and REENIE walk down the street. As REENIE turns up her music the banal movement of pedestrians organize themselves into visible counter-rhythms as REENIE takes it in. She can see patterns and affinities between unconnected people, a kind of harmony in shared space. REENIE begins to conduct the movement as if she has orchestrated this choreography. Now that she can see patterns, she seems to be summoning the movement.*

> *LIL and REENIE arrive home. REENIE sits on the couch, pulled into herself. LIL combs/twists REENIE's hair. We see some of REENIE's nerves draining away.*

Think about how much energy you're giving to negative thoughts, to doubting yourself, and how much you have left for, like, drawing pictures of yourself with biceps that defy physics.

REENIE: Stop looking at my notebook!

LIL: Stop leaving it open on the kitchen counter!

REENIE: And stop parenting so hard.

LIL: Soon as you stop childing.

REENIE: I won't.

LIL: Good. Don't. Wanna tell me a story?

REENIE: Which?

LIL: I thought they were announcing the recital piece today.

REENIE: Yeah. *The Firebird.*

LIL: Stravinsky?

REENIE: Yeah.

LIL: Oh, I like that one. All right, let's hear it.

REENIE: According to Maestra, it's a classic. A perfect piece to get us all noticed. Maestra says the soloist will have to embody the spirit of the firebird—a fierce and righteous protector of all the earth. So, the story: this is forever ago or whatever. In, like, Russia, I guess.

> *REENIE conjures the story, which is enacted fancifully by the other players. Casting is gender-irrelevant.*

There's this one fool named Koschei the Immortal, an ogre, who keeps his soul in an egg, in a casket, in a tree stump, for some reason. One day, this other fool named Prince Ivan, a hunter, wanders onto Koschei's land, sees this magnificent firebird, and captures it, instead of just minding his own business and moving on.

LIL: This feels editorialized . . .

REENIE: The story is always shaped by the teller, Mom. So, the firebird convinces Ivan to let her go by giving him a magical feather, even though the firebird owes Ivan nothing.

LIL: This is not at all how I learned it.

REENIE: Shh. Koschei's walking around his yard when he sees Ivan, the "hero," who is technically trespassing. Koschei is enraged; he sends all kinds of monsters and stuff to get Prince Ivan. But Ivan uses the feather to summon the firebird, who—although she still owes him nothing—makes Koschei and all the monsters dance an Infernal Dance, until they wear themselves out and fall asleep. The firebird shows Ivan the stump, with the casket, with the egg, with the soul in it.

LIL: I remember, from before.

REENIE: From before. Ivan destroys the egg, freeing all the enchanted beings across Koschei's land: birds, frogs, mongooses, and six princesses that I forgot to mention earlier. See, over time, Koschei had entrapped them all there, on his land, one by one, but suddenly the enchantment fell away. And the prince and princesses, birds, frogs, and mongooses all go off happily to wherever, while the righteous, powerful, and passionate firebird takes a bow, all the credit, and the title of the story, as if it's not perfectly obvious that Koschei was already half exhausted from the constant resistance of all those creatures in his captivity. So, really, they all did it.

The conjured re-enactment fades away.

LIL: Good story.

REENIE: Thanks. It's my gift. 'Kay, gotta go.

LIL: Go where?

REENIE: Into the darkness, to lurk.

REENIE opens her window to go out onto the fire escape.

LIL: Jacket, please.

REENIE drapes a light jacket over her shoulders. She poses heroically as the jacket cape flares out behind her.

Restraint

Ballet studio. Free hour before class. A dressmaker's judy has been set up next to a design sketch. MAIA, JO, and REENIE are working through a sequence. REENIE mimics MAESTRA.

REENIE: "Yes! Yes! Express the inexpressible. Inhabit the impossible!"

MAIA stops.

MAIA: Can you not?

REENIE: Chill out, Maia. We're supposed to be having fun, remember?

MAIA: Okay, have fun. Have fun in the background where no one can see you. Me and Jo don't wanna be stuck in Ensemble for the rest of our lives.

JO: Actually, I wouldn't mind / being in the back.

REENIE: Actually—

MAIA: Actually, me and Jo are aiming for something bigger. We're aiming for the solo, and we have a chance to get it.

JO: I like Ensemble. I like dancing with you all.

MAIA: So just reel it in, Reenie, and let us get through one sequence without a shenanigan.

REENIE: "Ooooh, look at me. I'm Maia. I take dancing super serious."

KARYN and DAWN enter and begin stretching.

MAIA: That's the truth. Now, brace me.

REENIE: 'Kay.

REENIE braces MAIA's leg for a deep stretch.

KARYN: Do these leg warmers make my legs look short? Maia?

DAWN: You have great legs, Karyn.

KARYN: Yeah, but can you see them?

DAWN experiments with rolling the leg warmers up/down for effect.

MAIA: Anyway, you should take this seriously too. You really do have a chance, you know.

REENIE: I know.

MAIA: I mean it. You could be the best . . . If I break both my legs and one of my arms falls off.

REENIE: Oh, it's like that? Race you to the barre!

MAIA: You're on!

*They race to the barre, laughing. MAESTRA enters and the
ensemble comes to attention.*

MAESTRA: We have a lot of work to do. I am not going to waste your
time—or mine. You are still in my class, that means I believe in you.
Prove me right.

*MAESTRA ceremoniously holds up a garment bag and removes an
ornate sash/cape, which is added to the judy. The first firebird reveal.*

You may respond.

ALL: Oooh!

REENIE: Miss, you know who would look really good in that? Admit
it. I'd look bomb.

MAESTRA: Ballet is not a fashion show, it's a calling. We have a system,
and we believe in the system because it works. The soloist will be
whomever can show me that they have the necessary talent, discipline,
and commitment. You must earn your place.

Now . . .

MAESTRA claps once. Ensemble takes position.

And . . .

MAESTRA claps twice, leads the class through "Sequence."

*Figures go past the classroom window. Time slows, light goes
buttery, MAESTRA and the ensemble stare. The older kids float
on easy laughter, impossibly wonderful and bathed in the glow*

*of superiority, riding currents of air like a gust of glitter and
bubbles. The class snaps back into real time when they go out
of view. The ensemble complete their piece. KARYN topples and
collides with REENIE, who pushes her away.*

KARYN: Ow! Reenie!

MAESTRA: Karyn. Pain is to be treated or endured, but never
spoken of.

REENIE: *(in ASL)* Sorry.

KARYN: *(in ASL)* No big deal.

> *MAESTRA holds the silence at the end of the sequence, then claps
> once. Ensemble takes position. MAESTRA goes down the line
> inspecting and correcting postures.*

Dawn, what are the permissible hairstyles?

DAWN: Ma'am. Bun, pony, French braid, pageboy.

MAESTRA: And what do you call that on your head?

DAWN: A . . . messy bun?

MAESTRA: Do you think there's room for mess in the ballet, Dawn?

DAWN: No, ma'am?

> *MAESTRA hands her a hairbrush. DAWN tightens up her bun.*

MAESTRA: Jo.

JO: Ma'am?

MAESTRA: Just . . . you're fine.

As MAESTRA approaches, KARYN sucks it in and up.

Karyn, keep it tucked in. Perfection does not wait until someone is watching. Maia, what is this?

MAIA: It's a bun, ma'am.

MAESTRA: No, this. All this.

MAIA: Braids . . .

MAESTRA: Oh?

MAIA: . . . In a bun.

MAESTRA: Unacceptable. Take them out.

MAIA: Out?

MAESTRA: Yes.

MAESTRA offers the brush. It hangs in the air.

MAIA: Ma'am, I can't.

MAESTRA: Because?

MAIA: It takes hours, ma'am.

MAESTRA: And?

MAIA: There's only ten minutes left in class.

MAESTRA: Then why haven't you begun?

> *MAESTRA snaps and points at MAIA. MAIA slowly takes down the bun and goes towards the corner with rigid control. MAESTRA claps the class back into "Sequence."*

(to herself, watching the class in the mirror) Yes, yes, yes! From these soggy little lumps of clay I will mould my masterpiece. Each one will be stretched, strained, and straightened out; cast by a master into superlative shape; pushed to surpass the possible and approach excellence.

> *MAESTRA turns back to the class and raises her voice.*

Continue to do your best, and then do better than that. The solo could still be yours, any one of you, so do not relent. Keep working. Keep pushing. Keep hoping.

> *LIL and POPS watch the class cool down through the window in the parents' waiting area.*

POPS: Wow. Your kid looks all right in there.

LIL: Yours, too. They've really been working hard.

POPS: Kids have no idea. Man, all this diversity stuff must be really good for her, huh?

LIL: . . . Yeah . . . It's good for Jo, too.

POPS: How so?

LIL exhales, smh.

MAESTRA: Inhabit the impossible, children! You are dismissed. Your free hour begins now.

MAESTRA claps once and exits.

POPS: Did Maestra say anything about the solo?

JO: It's too soon to know.

POPS: Give me one minute—

POPS starts into the studio. JO forestalls him.

JO: Dad, I'm super hungry.

POPS: You wanna go for burgers?

JO: I was thinking you could teach me how to barbecue.

POPS: Really? Today?

JO: Yeah. Unless this isn't barbecue weather.

POPS: Lesson one: it's always barbecue weather. You ready to do this?

JO: Totally!

POPS: All right.

JO: Okay.

POPS: Rahh!

JO: Rahh!

Movement: commute transition.

LIL and REENIE at home.
REENIE sits in lotus position, trying to cross every single part of her for good luck: fingers, toes, arms, legs, eyes. She strains audibly. LIL enters.

LIL: What are you doing?

REENIE: Hope, hope, hoping Maestra gives me the lead in *The Firebird*.

LIL: I was hoping you'd do the dishes last night. See where hope got me?

REENIE: Um, hope is only one of my many strategies.

LIL: Oh yeah? What else you got?

REENIE: As if you don't see me working on my arabesque while I brush my teeth.

LIL: I see you.

REENIE: Well then?

LIL: Imagine how good you'd be if you moved practise up from a side dish to the main course. You too good to try your best?

REENIE: No.

LIL: Good. What are you doing to move yourself out of the wings and into the spotlight?

REENIE: I dunno. It's dance, not math. Maestra already said that if I keep acting up I'm out of the running for lead. And I don't know if my sneezing fit counts against me—which I was NOT faking to get a laugh.

LIL: Your sneeze is pretty hilarious.

REENIE: I can't control what other people laugh at! Anyway, if that's acting up, then I might not get it, but I don't know if it is.

LIL: Have you thought of asking?

REENIE: Right, Mom. I'll just interrupt to ask if I'm on notice for interrupting.

LIL: Okay, obviously you can't speak in class. But you know, there's always at least . . .

REENIE: . . . At least three possible solutions to every problem.

LIL: And you always have / choices.

REENIE: You always have choices. Yeah. Such as?

LIL: You could wait for the right moment to talk to her.

REENIE: And die waiting? Pass.

LIL: Or you could create the right moment.

REENIE: What am I, a timelord?

LIL: Or you could skip the drama and focus on your dancing.

REENIE gives LIL the saltiest side-eye.

So what are you doing about it?

REENIE: Hello?! I'm hoping my butt off! I know I can play this part.

LIL: Well there's your problem. You're still trying to play the firebird. What you need to do is become the firebird.

REENIE: Yeah, okay. I'll do that.

LIL: No, you need to make Maestra see that you already are the firebird.

REENIE: Cool. So I'm thinking I'll spontaneously combust next week. Is that what you had in mind?

LIL: Aha. It becomes apparent that Maestra is not the problem here. How do you expect to convince her when you're not convinced?

REENIE: Mo-om.

LIL: Come on. Tell me one way you were amazing today.

REENIE: I'm not in the mood.

LIL: Then you'd better tell me two.

REENIE: Fine. Today I . . . parted my hair with perfect symmetry, all by myself. And I apologized to Karyn, even though she didn't ask me to, and even though we were both equally wrong, although if you think about it, she was a little more wrong than me.

LIL: Amazing! Now, let's see that rond de jambe. Who's the righteous protector of the earth?

REENIE goes through part of the routine, strengthening as she gains confidence.

REENIE: . . . Me?

LIL: Sho' nuff! Who's gonna light it up at that recital?

REENIE: Me, I guess.

REENIE's into a series of pirouettes now.

LIL: Who's the firebird?

REENIE: I am.

LIL: Who's the firebird?

REENIE: I am.

LIL: I can't hear you!

REENIE: I am!

LIL: Yeah, you are. Go on, girl. Get it.

Weaknesses

Movement: community. Family members are dropping off Junior Ensemble members at the studio. We can see that they are supported, invested, involved, proud.

Studio. MAIA intercepts MAESTRA at the door to discuss the hair situation. She still has her braids in. MAESTRA waves her off. MAESTRA claps once. Ensemble takes position. MAESTRA begins a line inspection.
REENIE runs in breathlessly, throws a bag in the corner, and takes her place.

MAESTRA: Reenie, you're late. Run a lap.

REENIE: Only five minutes!

MAESTRA: You want two? Rules are rules.

REENIE protests, silently, dramatically, then begins to run.

Do you even want this, Reenie?

REENIE: Like, the most?

DAWN: Ha ha!

MAESTRA: Okay, that's two laps for Dawn.

DAWN: Oh.

DAWN runs.

MAESTRA: Maia, what are you wearing? Where's your kit?

MAIA is silent.

Respond.

MAIA: I asked for help mending the hole, but my brother doesn't sew and my mom won't be back till Thursday—

MAESTRA: Concisely.

MAIA: I don't have it.

MAESTRA: Four laps. You know better. If you can't even get into proper kit, what hope do you have of grasping the ephemeral spirit of the moving body?

MAIA nods, steps back into line.

Be more than human. Be the dance.

MAESTRA claps once. Twice. They begin "Sequence."

Very good. Now I'd like to see the little section of the solo we worked on last week. Jo, Karyn, Reenie, line up. You too, Dawn. Maia, you can sit this one out.

MAIA: Why?

MAESTRA: *(exhales impatience)* Maia, the soloist will need parental permission. So there's no point—

MAIA: But, I have it.

MAESTRA: Your brother doesn't count, I'm afraid.

MAIA: I have the form. It's signed. By both of my parents, like you asked.

MAIA hands over the form.

MAESTRA: Oh. I see. Well, it looks like they didn't initial page two, so—

MAIA: I'll bring it back next week.

MAESTRA: All right, everyone.

MAESTRA claps once.

Karyn will begin.

KARYN: Miss—

MAESTRA: This is not a discussion!

KARYN begins the solo, feels all the eyes on her, runs out to puke. She returns partway through MAESTRA's next speech.

For some of you, the weaknesses will be *(ahem)* glaringly obvious. Others are more subtle. Remember, there are no small imperfections.

MAESTRA hands a folded page to each Ensemble member.

You've each got your own flaws, and that's where you need to spend your time. Use the extra studio time before and after class. I'm not here to hold your hand and make you feel safe. I'm here to challenge you and make you take risks. Now, these are your assessments. They are private, not to be shared. It's for you to work on you. Don't look to the others to make you stronger, you must bring your strongest self into the ensemble. You owe that to everyone in this room, and you should expect that from everyone in this room. And . . .

MAESTRA claps twice. The ensemble repeats a soft sequence, something lyric and tranquil. MAESTRA leads, then gets lost in the sequence. The class notices. MAESTRA covers her embarrassment with severity. MAESTRA claps once.

Adequate. Your free hour begins now.

MAESTRA exits. DAWN gets a juice box and spills it on her clothes.

DAWN: My mom says it's sad for those bullies that they feel the need to pick on me, but it doesn't help to give them a reason.

JO: Here, Dawn. Take this.

JO gives DAWN his jacket. DAWN ties it around her waist.

REENIE: Maia, can I see your leotard?

MAIA: It's just a little hole. It's not a big deal.

REENIE: I know, I just wanted to ask you a favor.

MAIA: Sure, what is it?

REENIE: Well, my mom wants me to practise sewing, so can I use this as my practice?

MAIA: I need to have it back by next week.

REENIE: You will, I promise.

MAIA: Well . . . all right, then.

MAIA takes up a space to work through the free hour. She reviews her assessment.

JO: Maia, we're all gonna meet at the arcade later. Wanna come?

MAIA: No thanks. Looks like I need the extra time.

MAIA begins to drill herself rigorously in her identified weakness.

REENIE: No you don't! You're nailing it! Now come nail the high score on *Toadblasters.*

MAIA: Reenie, your approval will mean so much more to me when you're running the class. But until then . . .

REENIE: Are you mad at me?

MAIA: Not at you.

REENIE: Okaaaay . . . Well as long as you're not mad, / how about—

MAIA: I don't wanna talk, Reenie. I'm losing minutes. The room's only free till seven.

REENIE: Okay, but I didn't do anything.

MAIA: Fine, Reenie. Just go.

REENIE: Not fine. What can I do?

MAIA: Shift left, Ree.

REENIE shifts left. MAIA continues.

REENIE: I'm on your side, Maia. How can she expect us to "move as one" when she makes us compete? Here, look at my assessment.

REENIE offers up her assessment. MAIA stops.

MAIA: That's private.

REENIE: Who cares? Look, I don't know why she's so hard on you in class. But I bet I got just as much criticism as you.

MAIA can't help but look. She takes out her own assessment to compare.

MAIA: Wait . . .

REENIE: See? She's just harsh. Transitions, weak. Extension, adequate. Arabesque, adequate.

MAIA: Wait, but your arabesque is terrible.

REENIE: So?

MAIA: So mine is perfect.

REENIE: No kidding. So?

MAIA: So how are we getting the same assessment? And how do you only have three "do betters," when I have seven?

REENIE: Wait, what? Oh. Weird. So . . . I'm gonna go. See you next week?

MAIA: Sure. Blast a toad for me.

REENIE: Pew pew.

MAIA is left alone and repeats the earlier soft sequence, but she tries to make it contain her anger, and it shows through—the piece is changed.

In the hall, LIL waits for REENIE. POPS and LIL have just arrived.

LIL: Your son is very generous.

POPS: Oh good. Now the world can eat him alive.

LIL: Wow. He must get it from his mother.

POPS: You know what? I'm doing my best. Is that all right with you?

LIL: I mean, we can all do better, am I right?

POPS: Geez. Jo! Let's go.

JO: But it's free hour.

POPS: You don't have to do that.

JO: Maestra says— *[that if we're committed . . .]*

POPS: First of all, they need you more than you need them.

JO: Yeah, but the others— *[are working on their . . .]*

POPS: Second, you're not like the others. Never forget that. Where's your jacket?

Movement: commute transition.

Home. REENIE alone.

REENIE goes through the motions, more marking than dancing. LIL enters and shakes her head. Through this scene, LIL and REENIE never face each other; one is always facing the other's back.

LIL: Inadequate, Reenie. Just inadequate.

REENIE: Oops! You weren't supposed to be watching.

LIL: Oops! I didn't know you only had to try when someone's watching. Now, where were you?

REENIE: Right about . . . here.

REENIE begins the sequence in earnest.

LIL: When I was your age, I'd be lucky to have enough living room to dance in, let alone any studio ensemble, Maestra. I taught myself.

LIL turns away. REENIE turns and begins to physically mimic LIL with inflated gestures, mouths the words—she's heard all this before.

You know what my mama would say if she found out I was fooling around during my lessons? Know what my mama would say? She'd say, "What lessons?" Know why? Cuz I didn't have any lessons.

LIL turns abruptly. REENIE turns too and snaps back into earnest dancing. LIL watches her, begins wistfully to mimic REENIE's solo. She performs a shadow duet with REENIE through the next text.

I learned by watching between backstage curtains, through rehearsal hall windows. I learned by wishing and then working towards that wish.

REENIE stops dancing and watches LIL solo.

I knew no one was gonna offer me a solo, but I danced . . . because . . .

LIL & REENIE: Because dancing is the most I/you ever mattered.

LIL: But seeing you up there is better than being there myself. So practise. Practise till it's instinct.

REENIE: No pressure. Mom, can you sew this for me?

LIL: This isn't one of yours.

REENIE: It's Maia's.

LIL: You've got a good heart.

REENIE: Aw shucks. I promised she could have it back by next week.

LIL: Meaning you promised I'd sew it by next week? But you know you can't make promises on behalf of other people.

REENIE: Please, Mom?

LIL: I'll do this, if you get back to doing that.

Outspoken

MAIA is drilling her weakness with her back to the room. The ensemble straggles in and begin warm-up. REENIE returns MAIA's leotard, holding it up for her to see, then dropping it near MAIA's bag.

MAIA: *(in ASL)* Thank you so much.

REENIE: *(in ASL)* No big deal.

KARYN: How was your assessment?

JO: Fine. Nothing I wasn't expecting.

REENIE: Did your dad see it?

JO: Yup.

KARYN: What did he say?

JO: "We are better than this!" He wasn't impressed.

REENIE: Shake it off. You're doing great, Jo.

JO: How about you, Dawn? You show yours to your mom?

DAWN: My mom says ballet costs about the same as babysitting but it has more structure, and I need structure, she says, so she doesn't mind how I do as long as I don't quit.

KARYN: Whoa.

JO: Must be nice.

KARYN: Maia, wanna warm up with us? Maia. Maia.

MAIA continues a repetitive cycle.

REENIE: She can't hear you, Karyn. She's a prisoner of the enchanted slippers of Mogazar, evil master of the dance.

JO: Should we go get help?

REENIE: No! She can only be released by a being pure of heart, chanting the abraxas. The words go . . . um . . .

JO: Mee-lah-bah-doo-zoh.

REENIE: Thank you, keeper of the abraxas.

JO: Milady.

DAWN: But which of us has a pure heart?

REENIE: No time to find out.

JO: We'll all have to do it together.

They advance on MAIA, chanting.

ALL: Mee-lah-bah-doo-zoh.

KARYN: Maia, come back!

As they near MAIA she turns suddenly and jump-scares the others.

MAIA: Maia's gone. I am Mogazar, evil master of the dance, and all shall do my will! Now . . .

MAIA claps once like MAESTRA. The ensemble gets in formation. MAIA claps again and inserts herself into the line. They begin. MAESTRA enters with a garment bag, stands near the judy, and awaits their complete attention. She pulls out a pair of wings and hangs them on the judy. MAESTRA signals permission for oohs and ahhs, then signals an end to oohs and ahhs. MAIA hands her an envelope.

Miss, my forms. Initialled on every page. By both parents.

MAESTRA: You don't really want the solo, Maia.

MAIA: I do. I really, really do.

MAESTRA: Solo's a lot of pressure, and you've already got so much going on.

MAIA: What do I have going on?

MAESTRA: You know . . . circumstances . . . life.

MAIA: Am I the only Ensemble member with a life?

MAESTRA: Just . . . get in line, Maia.

MAESTRA claps once. Ensemble takes position.

Remember: you are the grace in a disordered world.

MAESTRA claps twice. Ensemble begins "Sequence."

Movement: abbreviated or accelerated version of class.

Mid-sequence, REENIE causes a crack-up by imitating MAESTRA behind her back. MAESTRA waves it off.

MAIA: *(in ASL)* Stop it!

REENIE: *(in ASL)* What?!

MAESTRA: Maia. Focus please. And . . .

REENIE does it again.

Reenie! . . . Straighten that back leg.

REENIE does it again. It is obvious MAESTRA can see her.

MAIA: *(agog)* You all saw that! And then you're gonna try and tell me I don't get the solo because of a hole in my leotard?

MAESTRA: Maia, dance is about discipline. I'm afraid that little disruption is going to cost you.

MAIA: All right. All right, Reenie. I see you.

REENIE: Me?!

MAESTRA: Walk it off, Maia. In the hall.

MAIA balls up her sweater and throws it into the corner.

Come back in here when you can act more civilized. This is ballet, not basketball.

MAIA goes out into the hall to breathe it off. Class melts way.

Movement: city transition.

Home. REENIE and LIL. REENIE retells the classroom incident.

REENIE: Then she's like, "This is ballet, not basketball." The whole thing was just unbelievable!

LIL: Mm. What do you want for dinner?

REENIE: No, for real, though. Mom, I think Maestra's wrong.

LIL: About what? Is ballet the same as basketball?

REENIE: I don't think anyone else should take the part if Maia really earned it.

LIL: M'kay, correction: you wouldn't be taking it, you would be receiving it. Maestra would be giving it to you.

REENIE: So . . . it's okay for me to take the win, even if someone else is cheating?

LIL: Huh? No!

REENIE: Then how would that be okay?

LIL: Because this will pass. There will be other things for Maia. And the struggle will make her strong.

REENIE: Oh, okay. Good for future Maia. Until then, here's what it's gonna be like for present-day Reenie:

There I am, standing at centre stage. I look good. Maia's in the background with the others. Oh, how lovely. All the pretty dancers in their places. I feel a slight prickly heat on the back of my neck, a spreading warmth, then a burning sensation from Maia's laser eyes drilling a hole right through me as this injustice awakens inside of her an unimaginable power beyond her control. Lasers are shooting out all over the stage! The curtain goes up in flames, babies are crying in the balcony, a man in the front row faints, then one of the lasers burns into the audience, grazing the edge of a velvet seat in row L. Oh, no! My mom's sitting in row L! It's all happening so fast, there's nothing I can do. Oh, well. You're incinerated. Now I have to stay with Shauna forever, an orphan, eating Tofurky at Christmas. Is that what you want? Because that's what will happen.

LIL: What do you want me to say?

REENIE: Don't say anything. Do something.

LIL: Maia's not getting that part.

REENIE: Yeah, I know she's not. Get this. So after, Maestra pulls me aside and says not to even worry about it. Maia's gotta get over it if she wants to be part of this ensemble. Dancers need a thick skin.

LIL: See, I tell you that all the time—

REENIE: She says Maia just isn't solo material.

LIL: I'm sure she has her reasons . . .

REENIE: Cuz her look is too urban to play the lead in a classic. Too. Urban. Unbelievable!

LIL: I don't get it, Reenie.

REENIE: What don't you get? I was like, "Not cool, man."

LIL: Reenie . . . do you want to be that girl?

REENIE: The one who's always right?

LIL: The fighty one. The one who can't pick her battles. Dance is about discipline. Is this worth it?

REENIE: Oh, come on, Mom.

LIL: I'm coming. Take me there.

REENIE: All right, what do you think Maestra means by "urban"?

LIL: How should I know?

REENIE: Because you live in the world, and you know what words mean.

LIL: Let's all just check our tone a little.

REENIE: Sorry.

LIL: I think Maestra knows what she's doing.

REENIE: Oh, okay. So did you also agree with coach last year when he said that I'm too fragile to try out for football?

LIL: Can we have one grievance at a time, please?

REENIE: Mom, you know she's good.

LIL: Fine, she's good.

REENIE: She's as good as me. Better.

LIL: You can't say that. It's dance, not math, Reenie.

REENIE: She's definitely good enough to dance the solo.

LIL: So are you.

REENIE: But I don't come early, stay late, or refrain from foolishness.

LIL: Look, I watched you reaching for this. I watched you rehearse and sweat and improve. And unlike some people, you've got a mom who's willing to put in the time to support you. What's your complaint again?

REENIE: Ugh. You don't get anything.

LIL: I really don't, Reenie. Dance is competitive. That means someone wins, and a whole lot of folks don't. This time, Maia doesn't.

REENIE: Even though she never messes up! Maestra's being stupid.

LIL: Eh!

REENIE: Sorry. But this is supposed to be about talent, discipline, and commitment. If doing literally everything right to the point that you are annoying, if all that gets you nowhere, why would anyone even try?

LIL: Because being the best is for yourself. It's not about the rules or the system.

REENIE: Wait, there's a whole system?

LIL: What? No! I'm saying you have to do your best, but it's not all about the win.

REENIE: So, what I'm hearing is, you don't mind if I break the rules, as long as I'm being my best self?

LIL: You know I'm not / saying that—

REENIE: Oh, okay. So you're saying I shouldn't expect anything to come from trying hard or doing good.

LIL: Reenie, / that's not what I—

REENIE: And you're saying it's okay that it's unfair, because dance is unfair, so get used to it!!

LIL: I'm saying... that ... Maestra has to consider a lot of different factors that you're not even aware of. Maybe if you knew them, you'd realize it's more fair than you think.

REENIE: Ohhh, okay. It's secretly fair. That makes sense.

LIL: Are you asking me to talk to Maestra about this?

REENIE: No.

LIL: Are you going to talk to Maestra yourself?

REENIE: I'd rather not.

LIL: Do you want to stop taking the class?

REENIE: No!

LIL: Then what do you want?

REENIE: I want to win. But only because I'm actually the best, not just because I'm the one with acceptable hair.

LIL: Sometimes it's like that, baby. There's a time and a place to make noise. You have such big emotions, Reenie. That's the dance in you. You gotta put it back into the dance.

REENIE: Really? Did you just tell me to shut up and dance?

LIL exhales with control.

LIL: Reenie, there are bigger problems in this world than too much winning.

REENIE: THIS IS BIG! THIS IS REALLY BIG! TO ME. TO ME.

LIL: Know what, Reenie? I'm tired. Why don't you go out for a walk?

REENIE: How's a walk gonna help?

LIL: You're right. Better make it a run.

REENIE: Ugh.

REENIE heads for the door.

LIL: Reenie!

REENIE turns back, petulantly.

REENIE: What?

LIL: Take a water bottle. Stay hydrated.

LIL & REENIE: Water is life.

LIL waits until REENIE leaves the room, then dials the phone.

LIL: . . . I'd like to speak with Maestra, please. This is Lil, Reenie's mom. Yes, I'll hold.

REENIE is running all out. She hits that spot where exertion allegedly feels good.

Movement: training.

REENIE: It's hard and it's hard and it's hard, then suddenly you're on the other side and your body says, "Yes, look what I can do." It's good when you hit your stride, but it's even better when you hit the wall, and you can't possibly go on, but you do anyway. You find some way to keep pushing, and it feels right, having something to push against, to push through. The wall's not there to stop you, it's where you level up. It's where you prove how much you want it.

The following section is interspersed with LIL's *call.*

I was born to go there. I was born to push, to win. My mama raised me to be a winner. / I'm not a quitter. I'm not a pushover. I'm a winner. / There's nothing I can't do. / There's no wall I can't get over.

LIL: Maestra? Yes, I'm fine. How are you? / I understand you're still considering the solo assignment, but I was wondering, have you considered a firebird lead . . . duet? / Who cares if there's no glory in duets? It's a year-end recital, not an Olympic tryout. / I see. No, I understand. Of course I want her to take it seriously . . . Yes, she certainly does have a lot of spirit. Thank you.

> REENIE *returns from running, runs into her room, and slams the door.* LIL *hears the window open as* REENIE *goes out onto the fire escape.*

> REENIE *reaches back for a scarf, ties it around her head like the Karate Kid, and strikes a power pose.*

Collusion

Ballet studio.

Prior to class. REENIE *rallies the class and speechifies, steamrolling the tentative interjections of others.*

REENIE: . . . And that's when we spring it on her. At the recital, right before we go on stage. She'll be all, like, "Children!" But it's too late to stop us, and the whole show gets turned upside down. Cuz a system only works if all of the parts in it work. We may be in it, but we don't have to work with it.

Cuz we're an ensemble, right? / Right.

KARYN: Yeah, right / but . . .

REENIE: That means we stick together, right? / Right.

JO: Uh, / yeah . . .

REENIE: All for one and one for all, right? / Right.

DAWN: Sure, I / guess . . .

REENIE: The great thing about my plan is it makes the ballet even better—fresher!

MAIA: How does this / make it better?

REENIE: Okay. Great.

KARYN: I have questions . . .

REENIE: Glad we had this talk. I'll tell you more after class.

MAESTRA enters with a hat box, extracts the firebird headpiece.
KARYN gets the vapours.

MAESTRA: One of you will rise above the others. One of you will be my firebird. My masterpiece. A blazing star, who will etch my name into the sky. I will elevate you to unknown heights, and you will say, "I am the firebird. Maestra made me." Tell that to the dean.

Come here, Karyn. Try this on for me, just to see it.

KARYN: Miss?

KARYN tries on the headpiece. MAESTRA considers her in it.
Everyone does. After a moment, KARYN wants to take it off.
MAESTRA removes it from her head and puts it atop the judy.
Class begins.
MAESTRA claps once. Ensemble takes their positions.
MAESTRA claps twice. "Sequence" begins. Ensemble
engulfs MAESTRA in a firestorm cyclone throughout the next
speech.

The Firebird will be the pinnacle, the peak of Junior Ensemble accomplishments. It is ambitious, unheard of. This is going to get us noticed, and getting noticed is how you get ahead. It is a mark of excellence, then you won't be stuck here, dealing with these undisciplined limbs and unformed minds anymore; then you'll face real challenges, because once they move you up, you'll be rid of these entitled amateurs. Instead, you will be teaching an aspiring ensemble of dedicated pre-professionals, the beautiful stars with their long, lithe limbs ready to be shaped into the vision you demand with rigour! Passion! Perfection!

MAESTRA turns back to the class.

Do you hear that, children? Rigour! Passion! Perfection! It has to be perfect or none of us are going anywhere!

MAESTRA claps once.

All right that's it for today. Free hour begins now.

MAESTRA exits. REENIE summons Ensemble members over and opens her stuffed bag. She takes out a hoodie and holds it out to JO while digging out another.

REENIE: And now for part two of my plan. Here, this should fit you. I think it's the smallest one. They're not all the same colour, but a hoodie's a hoodie, so . . .

No one takes a hoodie. REENIE is left hanging. She eventually notices and stops rummaging, looking up. Everyone is looking away from her.

We have to practise in them at home, or it'll feel weird dancing in them at the recital.

No takers.

JO: The costumes are really good this year.

REENIE: Yes, and you're going to wear them. Under these. We'll show Maestra who's "urban."

JO: I guess . . .

REENIE: Dawn?

DAWN: What if we get kicked out?

REENIE: Oh, as if. That's not gonna happen.

DAWN: My mom says it's really important for me to participate in activities with kids my own age and I already washed out of gymnastics and tae kwon do.

REENIE: Karyn?

KARYN: We worked so hard to get clean lines. Who's gonna see them in these?

REENIE: Wow, really? No one?

Still, no one is moving. She appeals to MAIA.

Really, Maia? After all my— After all your work and sacrifice. Are you gonna let Maestra get away with this?

MAIA: I didn't ask for any of this. Forget it, Reenie. Thanks, anyways.

REENIE stares everyone down. She paces. It's awfully quiet.

REENIE: Okay. If Maia doesn't want to do it . . .

MAIA: I don't.

REENIE: Okay. Then, okay.

> *REENIE turns away, disappointed. LIL and POPS arrive.*
> *Ensemble members collect their things and leave. Focus: JO stays*
> *behind for free hour. POPS moves towards the studio. LIL grabs*
> *his arm and holds him back. POPS watches JO, relaxing against*
> *the door frame, proud.*

> *Movement: JO spotlight.*

JO: Not everybody needs to stand out. By yourself, you are just your-self. But somehow it is possible to give yourself to this bigger thing and then you see it, and it is beautiful and big, and it is something you could never have done by yourself, but you also see how it couldn't happen without you, so you are that big, beautiful thing that is bigger and better than you ever could be. Even if you make a mistake, even if you're not the best, it doesn't matter because it's not about you; you're part of a much bigger picture. You're not alone. Everyone is holding each other up. You're together, and together you're strong.

> *JO sees POPS watching and the spell breaks. JO stops dancing and*
> *gets his bag. POPS straightens up and returns to his "normal."*

POPS: Let's go! Let's go!

JO: Going!

POPS: Hey, tuck your shirt in. Don't be common.

> *REENIE and LIL, almost home.*

LIL: What happened?

REENIE: Nothing. Forget it.

LIL: All right.

REENIE: Thanks.

LIL: So . . .

REENIE: So . . .

LIL: So, pineapple smoothie?

REENIE: . . . Yeah.

LIL: Cool.

A smoothie vendor appears and begins blending.

REENIE: Mom, I think I'm gonna skip the next class.

LIL: No, I think you're not.

REENIE: But there's a comicon in town, and it's only that weekend!

LIL: There's a what? I don't even care. You're important to the team, Reenie. Why would you start slacking off now?

REENIE: Ho-lee! Do I need to spend my whole entire life doing the first thing I'm good at? Anyways, would it kill them to rehearse without me one time?

LIL: Reenie, you're in an ensemble, and I know you know what that means. You all have to get stronger together. What are they supposed to do if you're not there? Dance around the gap? No, I don't think so. Did I make this commitment?

REENIE: No.

LIL: Who made this commitment?

REENIE: I did.

LIL: You did. And?

REENIE: And I'll see it through.

LIL: Yeah, you will.

REENIE: And I'm adding raspberries.

LIL: Yeah, you are.

> *REENIE takes out a comic book. LIL smooths down REENIE's hair. REENIE leans into her. LIL gets a text. She hands REENIE some money.*

All right, I'm gonna go ahead. Meet me at home. Be safe.

REENIE: Mom, it's two blocks.

LIL: And don't get distracted. You're being picked up in half an hour.

> *Movement: commute transition.*

Reenie Is Kept Waiting

REENIE looks at her watch and jumps over to the couch, where she sits with a bag in her lap. Time lapse.
LIL passes through the room, very casually.

LIL: Wanna watch a movie?

REENIE: No thanks.

LIL passes through again, casually, checks for a text on her way out.

LIL: I'm making myself a hot chocolate. Want one?

REENIE: He'll be here soon.

LIL: I know.

REENIE takes out a book and starts doodling.

Can I sit with you while you wait?

REENIE: Yeah.

LIL gets behind REENIE and wraps her up.

LIL: Who's this?

REENIE: His name is Reliable Man. He has the power to be in two places at once, so he never lets anyone down.

LIL: Unless he's promised to be in three places.

REENIE: Why would he do that?

LIL: Some people have trouble recognizing their limitations.

REENIE: I wouldn't know. I don't have any. I'm gonna give him a watch. So he knows when he's late.

LIL: You're so talented it's scary, you know that?

REENIE: Thanks, Mom.

> *REENIE leans into LIL and keeps drawing. LIL extracts herself and goes into the kitchen.*

Mom. Mom! Is that hot chocolate still a thing? Mom?

Do You

Pre-class. REENIE catches up with MAIA.

REENIE: Maia! I have another great idea.

MAIA: Good luck with that.

REENIE: Ha ha. Anyways, listen. This one is epic. Colossal. Unignorable.

MAIA: Is this new idea about how we can get more rehearsal time, and therefore become better dancers? Cuz I'm into that plan.

REENIE: What? Ha! No. Quite the opposite. Do you know what a boycott is? It's when you agree to not do something. Next week, Maestra shows up to an empty class. The dean's all like, "Maestra, where's all your students at?" and Maestra's like, "Uhhh," and she looks like the world's worst teacher.

MAIA: So, I don't get it. What's your end game here? To get her fired? You want us to have no teacher?

REENIE: No, I just . . . I—

MAIA: You wanna have no classes?

REENIE: I wouldn't go / that far—

MAIA: Because if that's what you want, seems like it would be easier to quit than to drag us all into your thing.

REENIE: And how would that lead to big change?

MAIA: Why do you feel the need to be noticed all the time?

REENIE: Why are you so afraid to be noticed?

MAIA: Why should I be?

REENIE: Um, cuz you deserve it? You're the best in the whole school.

MAIA: *(brake screech)* No, I'm not. Not yet. But I will be, if I focus and keep working, if you stop constantly distracting me. Do you know how few people make it in this thing? I am going to make it. I am.

REENIE: Oh for sure, but that doesn't mean you can't also—

MAIA: No. I got no time for "also," Reenie. I am here to dance. I choose to be here, and I'm gonna do what Maestra says, because I am here to learn. What are you here for?

REENIE: I'm . . . here to be my best self.

Ensemble members begin to straggle in.

MAIA: Then do that. You don't need my help, or my permission. You don't need any of us. People will move when they are moved. Stop pushing us around and go do you. I'm saying this with love. Now, can you brace me?

REENIE: Sure.

REENIE braces MAIA for a deep stretch.

I'll always support you, Maia.

MAIA: Even if we disagree?

REENIE: Even if.

MAIA: Big talk, Ree.

REENIE: Big love, Maia.

MAIA: I hear that. Big love back. Even though we disagree.

REENIE drops the leg.

REENIE: Disagree about what?

MAIA: For starters, *Toadblasters* is a baby game for babies.

REENIE: Oh really!

MAIA: Really.

REENIE: I guess I'd think that too if I knew I couldn't touch the high score.

REENIE resumes bracing MAIA's leg.

DAWN: Can you show me the fouetté again?

KARYN: Sure.

KARYN demonstrates. DAWN poorly emulates her.

DAWN: Was that one?

KARYN: Kind of. Except not. Forget gravity exists. Just float it.

DAWN: It's hopeless. I can't do it.

MAESTRA enters.

MAESTRA: Dawn! You absolutely can do it. Don't ever let me hear you expressing doubt like that again.

MAESTRA claps once. Ensemble takes up positions.

Some of you believe that you can't do this. You are mistaken. Kindly conceal your ignorance. The soloist will be selected next week. Earn it.

MAESTRA claps twice. "Sequence," at high speed.

LIL watches through the window in the parents' waiting area. POPS arrives.

POPS: They almost done?

LIL: Any second now.

POPS: Good. Weekends are such a hustle.

LIL: Tell me about it.

POPS: Hey, have you seen the firebird costume?

LIL: It's beautiful.

POPS: It is. And it's expensive.

LIL: Oh, yeah.

POPS: Twice as much as the ensemble costume.

LIL: Duly noted.

POPS: Just something to think about.

DAFONTE: Mm. You know the soloist also has to show up for a lot of extra rehearsals, so . . .

POPS: So?

DAFONTE: Just so many things to think about.

JO comes out from the studio.

POPS: Hey, buddy.

JO: I'm coming.

POPS: You, uh, have a good time in class today?

JO: Why are you being weird?

POPS: No, I'm not. Get out of here.

JO obeys. POPS regrets saying that.

No, I didn't mean—why are you so sensitive?

JO: I'm sorry.

POPS: Jo, I'm here to help you. You know that, right?

JO: Help me with what?

POPS: With whatever. To succeed. To win.

JO: What if I want to succeed at being in the ensemble?

POPS: You need to shoot higher than that, buddy.

JO: So not "whatever," then.

POPS: One day, when you least expect it, no matter how hard you try, someone's gonna pull the rug out from under you, and I'm the one who's gonna be here to pick you up.

JO: Dad . . . You gotta get back up. You gotta move on. You can't spend every minute expecting the worst. I can't.

POPS: I don't want you to expect the worst, Jo. I want you to be ready for it. You can't understand right now, but you will.

JO: Dad, what if I'm not ready for the solo?

POPS: What does Maestra know?

JO: No, what if I don't feel ready?

POPS: Uhhh. I dunno, Jo. We'll talk about it later. Burgers?

JO: Sure, Dad.

Focus; MAIA is rehearsing/working out. DAWN and KARYN are also using the extra hour.

Movement: commute transition.

REENIE: 'Kay, I did the dishes and I'm all packed for tomorrow. I'll be outside, lurking.

LIL: Hold it.

REENIE: What? I already did my homework.

LIL: What's that funny bulge in your dance bag?

REENIE: Nothing, warden. Just a rope and a grappling hook to get over that there wall, and a couple of raw steaks to distract the dogs.

LIL: Reenie . . .

REENIE: What?

LIL: Stop being clever. Just tell me. Is there tomfoolery in that bag?

REENIE: Why am I suddenly under suspicion? This is totally profiling.

LIL: Girl, I never saw anyone work so hard to sabotage what they spent all year reaching for.

REENIE: Mom, the way I see it, I've got at least three choices. I can pretend I don't see what's going on. I can admit I see it and agree to be a part of it. Or I can make it stop.

LIL: Reenie, I hope you don't go and do anything you're gonna regret.

REENIE: I am the firebird. Just like you said, Mom.

LIL: You are, baby.

REENIE: I am righteous, passionate, fierce. I am a protector of the earth.

LIL: And that's why you have to dance it.

REENIE: That's why I can't. Mom, Maia really wants this. Like, reeee-allly wants it—and she deserves it. I just like winning. Maia feels like she matters when she dances. I feel that way all the time—you make me feel that way, all the time. I matter. Now, can you be proud of me for letting this be someone else's moment?

LIL: Did I ever tell you about the last time I danced?

REENIE: Only a million times. Tell me again.

LIL: We were dancing *Giselle*. I was Ensemble in this wee little company, and we were in dress rehearsals. There was this one turn I couldn't get. Ever. I finally decided that if I couldn't do a quarter turn to the left, I would just do a three quarter turn to the right. So I turned right . . .

REENIE: . . . Right into the pit.

LIL: Right. Into. The pit. And my last dance was your first. You were already growing inside of me and I wasn't about to take another chance like that. Cuz you mean more to me than anything. Think of that.

REENIE: I am.

LIL: You are a part of me, and dance is a part of you.

REENIE: I get it.

LIL: Think of how hard I had to fight for the little I had, the legacy I left you. Think of my last dance, and your granny's squinty eye. Remember it's not just you up there, it's all of us.

REENIE: No pressure.

LIL: Well, whatever you do, you're the one that has to live with it.

REENIE: Exactly. And not just me. Mom, what if, back then when you were fighting for your chance, what if someone had fought for you? Or what if you didn't have to fight at all; what could we be? I could be a quarterback!

LIL: Everybody's fighting something, Ree.

REENIE: Have some imagination, Mom. You're not supposed to get used to a wrong thing. Or is that what you want me to do? Get used to it? Be part of it? Mind my own business?

LIL: I dunno, Reenie. I really don't.

REENIE: I'm going outside. See you in a bit.

LIL: See you, little girl.

REENIE goes onto the fire escape.

Reenie, it's dark out there.

LIL follows and hands her a flashlight. REENIE lightsabers the air with sound effects. REENIE shuts off the flashlight. They look at the sky.

REENIE: You ever heard of light pollution? Turns out you have to stop shining to see the real stars.

Back All The Way Up

Ballet studio before class.
REENIE rabble-rouses, with interjections from Ensemble,
minus MAIA.

REENIE: All right, I get it. There's a system.

ALL: Yes. / Right.

REENIE: And you believe in the system. And you want to work within the system.

ALL: Yes. / Exactly.

REENIE: And you don't want to blow it up . . .

ALL: NO!

REENIE: . . . For some reason.

ALL: REENIE! / Geez!

REENIE: Jo, do you want the solo?

JO: No!

REENIE: Right. Karyn, if you get the solo, is your stomach gonna make it to opening?

KARYN: Probably not.

REENIE: Right. Dawn, do you even care?

DAWN: Don't you?

REENIE: Of course I do. But I don't want it like this. I don't want it enough to be someone I don't like. I'm better than that. Are you?

ALL: Yes.

REENIE: Okay.

JO: Okay, so we're all pure of heart. Now what? In forty seconds, Maestra is gonna come in here and name the soloist. Do we chant the abraxas, or . . . ?

REENIE: Listen, the best of us should get the solo. We can all agree on that. And according to the system, that means whoever shows discipline, passion, precision—and pure skills. I think we all know who that describes. Maybe Maestra just needs a little help to see it. Maybe we need to amplify what's already there.

> *REENIE removes a forearm cast from her bag and puts it on one of her arms. MAIA enters and stretches. MAESTRA enters. Claps once. Only MAIA and KARYN get in line. MAESTRA claps once again. DAWN hurries into line.*

DAWN: Sorry, miss!

MAESTRA: Shh!

MAIA: *(in ASL)* What are you doing?

MAESTRA claps twice. JO faces backwards absurdly.

MAESTRA: Jo!

MAIA: Jo!

JO turns to face front. "Sequence" begins.

REENIE: How does this go again?

MAESTRA: Reenie!

MAIA: Oh, come on!

KARYN dances in slow motion. MAESTRA turns off the music.

MAESTRA: I have never seen such a stunning display of incompetence in all my years. Today, of all days! I'm disappointed in all of you.

REENIE & MAIA: All of us?

They all look at MAIA.

MAIA: Hold on. Do you think I can only win if you get out of the way? This is very nice. You're good friends, really. But I didn't come here to play nice with my friends. I came here to be the best, and right now, in this class, I am. But if you think you're the one, come test me.

MAESTRA: We have rules, Maia.

MAIA: Yeah, I know, and according to your rules, I've earned the solo. My legs are strong, made for this, and I feel myself getting stronger all the time. My spirit is opened up when I dance. It's better than flying, or swimming, or running, better than winning. It's all of those things and it's more than that. It's like my whole entire body is a bright, burning flame that warms the room, and that is something I have, something I can give, something that can open up other people's spirits, make other people want to do whatever it is they need to do. Make them remember the ways that they are strong, and capable, and beautiful, too. I want to be good enough to give them that. I am the firebird. So it's up to you. Do you want to be charitable and give Karyn a chance to take it from me?

MAESTRA: I have already decided . . . I had already planned to allow you to compete. That was my plan, that I planned already. After all, you must earn your place. Karyn will begin.

KARYN is already sick. She's out.

Karyn! What in the world—

MAIA: Like you said, solo's a lot of pressure. Good thing some of us are used to pressure. Cuz of life. And circumstances. The solo section. Let's go. Music.

MAESTRA: Maia, I'm still in charge here. Music!

MAIA: That's what I'm talking about.

REENIE: You know I want this. Same as you.

REENIE removes the cast from her arm.

MAIA: So come get it.

REENIE: You're on!

All line up and begin to dance the solo section. The rest are equal for half a minute, then the intricacy picks up.

JO: Ow, ow, ow.

MAIA: If you can't take it . . .

DAWN drops out.

REENIE: Bring it, Maia!

MAESTRA claps thrice. All break into free dance.

MAIA: Whooo!

MAESTRA claps twice. They return to the routine.

JO: Where are we?

JO doubles back on the choreo, sees his error, drops out.

REENIE: Come on. Where we going?

MAIA: Let's see if you can keep up.

LIL arrives and watches through the window. MAIA begins to modify the routine. REENIE follows her lead. The dance is energetic, frenzied, balletic, and I dare say even a bit urban. REENIE drops out, watching MAIA with open admiration. The ensemble playfully reprise their roles as freed captives from The Firebird, *and eventually adorn* MAIA *with the accoutrement, except the headpiece, which* MAESTRA *has snatched up.*

POPS arrives outside the studio.

POPS: What's going on?

LIL: Looks like Maestra's ready to assign the solo.

POPS: Move out of my way.

DAFONTE: Leave them.

POPS: If you think I'm gonna let you / *[stop me]*—

DAFONTE: Let? What "let"? No one's asking your permission. This doesn't involve you.

POPS: Of course it does. That's my son. We're legacy. We made this place.

LIL: Well I'm a mom and that's my amazing kid and her incredible friends down there. Now, please excuse me while I watch my daughter make me proud.

The ensemble is now in full swing, MAIA *as firebird, the others in support.* MAESTRA *is loving it.*

POPS: You don't corner the market on being proud.

LIL: Does Jo know?

POPS: Sure, but some kids / need *[a different]*—

LIL: Our kids have just as much legacy as your son. We made this, too.

LIL and POPS stand there awkwardly waiting, distinctly separate, LIL between POPS and the door. REENIE greets LIL silently before they exit. JO emerges from the studio.

POPS: If you want it, I'll get you that solo.

JO: How about you don't.

POPS: I'm trying to understand you, but how are you gonna get what you want if you can't even say it?

JO: I said it, Dad. Maybe you need to hear. I'm in the car.

POPS considers going into the studio, but doesn't.

POPS: I'm coming.

JO exits. POPS follows. MAESTRA puts the firebird headpiece on MAIA's head. They both turn towards the mirror.

MAESTRA: Brava, ma petite. Brava.

MAIA accepts this with a nod. MAESTRA signals free hour and leaves. MAIA begins warming up into the solo. This continues through to the end.

Movement: commute transition.

Home. REENIE and LIL go to the fire escape and look out over the city. A denouement.

LIL: Sorry you didn't get the win this time.

REENIE: I got exactly what I wanted.

LIL: Hm. Okay. So, now what do you wanna do with your weekends? Swimming? Animation? Cure sickle cell anemia?

REENIE: How about . . . ballet?

LIL: Really?

REENIE: Really. You know what dancing feels like. Would you wanna stop?

LIL and REENIE dance a soft duet together.

Below them, MAIA stays shining.

Fin.

Donna-Michelle St. Bernard, a.k.a. Belladonna the Blest, is an emcee, playwright, and agitator. Her main body of work, the 54ology, includes *Cake, Sound of the Beast, A Man A Fish, Salome's Clothes, Gas Girls, Give It Up, The Smell of Horses*, and *The First Stone*. Works for young audiences include the META-nominated *Reaching For Starlight, The Chariot*, and *Rabbit King of Kenya*. Opera libretti include *Forbidden* (Afarin Mansouri/ Tapestry Opera) and *Oubliette* (Ivan Barbotin/Tapestry Opera). She is co-editor with Yvette Nolan of the Playwrights Canada Press *Refractions* anthologies, and editor of *Indian Act: Residential School Plays*.